Love Nailed to the Doorpost

Love Nailed to the Doorpost

POEMS

Richard Chess

University of Tampa Press

Manufactured in the United States of America
Printed on acid-free paper ∞
First Edition

On the Cover:
Daniel Nevins, "C'mon, Lazarus" (2016), oil and acrylic on wood, 30 x 24 inches.

Cover design by Joshua Steward and Richard Mathews

The University of Tampa Press
401 West Kennedy Boulevard
Tampa, FL 33606

ISBN 978-159732-146-4 (hbk.)
ISBN 978-159732-145-7 (pbk.)

Browse & order online at
http://utpress.ut.edu

Library of Congress Cataloging-in-Publication Data

Names: Chess, Richard, author.
Title: Love nailed to the doorpost : poems / Richard Chess.
Description: First edition. | Tampa, FL : University of Tampa Press, [2017]
Identifiers: LCCN 2017001711 | ISBN 9781597321464 (hardback : acid-free paper) | ISBN 9781597321457 (paperback : acid-free paper)
Classification: LCC PS3553.H42 A6 2017 | DDC 811/.6--dc23
LC record available at http://lccn.loc.gov/2017001711

Contents

IV. What I've Been Given

For Laurie, Alice, Margaret, and Gabe—written into *this* book of life

I. Love Nailed Slant

The Other Face of Adam

When Adam saw her, muscle of a new day,
when he squatted to smell the musk
between her legs, when he leaned down

To grasp the wrist of the most familiar
creature he'd encountered yet, to pull
himself, the mirror image of himself, to her feet;

When he took a few steps back
to appraise her with the mind of sun,
the heart of moon, to praise her

With the applause of leaves bestirred,
to seduce her with the iridescence
of lizard skin, to navigate into the current of her

And power through her like a fish
through a diaphanous river's shadow and light,
to know her with every cell, every molecule, all

The elements that spun into his inception—
when he stood back from her again
with all creation

Pulsing in his temples, with his unique
talent, endowed in him by his creator, to see
beyond the moment's garden

All the way into the biomedical engineer's lab,
suddenly he understood the world
would never culminate nor close with him

And he was frightened, the first, the original
terror which he couldn't tell from wonder
as he stood there regarding what was made

Of the same stuff as he yet utterly strange—
how the world around him even then
was tossing up difference after difference,

Until maybe even they'd be tossed aside
should this new allowance for difference
not grow the way god dreamed it would

When god dreamed Eve through Adam into being.

I Lied

I lied. I didn't lie. Someone close, very close to me lied.

The lie was part heritage, part invention. She came from a line of liars. On her mother's side. That's what her mother told her. Her mother never lied to me, so she must have been telling the truth to her daughter.

She lied about the last 30 minutes of her life, the ride from the airport. Behind that lie was another, the lie of the five hours before that.

She was hungry, so she ate while she lied. She laughed and she ate and she lied her way through the meal and the lie flew with her, spicy and fresh as the taste of ginger in her mouth, to Peru.

Does it matter who she lied to? Does it matter that she lied, at that meal, to her grandmother, the only surviving member of the generation through whom the lie passed down to her?

She didn't lie. I lied. She didn't eat with her grandmother that night. Her mother, my wife, did. She ordered an Appletini. No, that was her mother. My wife's mother ordered the Appletini.

My wife was tense as she constructed a lettuce wrap and ate it. She knew she had to be careful. Careful about what she said in response to her mother's questions.

Her mother asked, where did you fly from. Her mother asked, where are you staying while you are here. Her mother asked, is he working this summer. Her mother asked, when is the baby due, where is the wedding going to be, why wasn't I told sooner, why wasn't I the first to know.

She wasn't alone with her mother. All the years were with them at the table, and the crispy honey shrimp. She didn't exactly lie to her mother, but she didn't answer fully any of her mother's questions. She couldn't. She couldn't because of what happened in Haddonfield, how her mother treated her when she was a girl, and she couldn't because of what happened in Hollywood, when she sent one of her own daughters to visit grandma, and then the other daughter, and then her son.

She couldn't because she wasn't there that night. She didn't crack open the cookie, receive the fortune: "Adventure can be a real happiness". I lied.

Lying can be an adventure. Like examining patients in rural Uganda: a stop on a residency tour. The comforts of home—the electrical outlet, the exterminator—beyond reach. To survive, you must adjust. You must make do.

And you do. The lie is the risk you take for family. *L'dor v'dor*: from generation to generation, the lie binds mother to daughter, father to son. A spirited song, with gusto you sing it.

The lie is intimate, and the lie is personal, a gift from your heart, a small masterpiece of narrative art.

Here's the truth: it was me at that dinner. I was alone. I always eat alone.

There was someone else at the table, maybe more than one other guest: my mother-in-law, my brother-in-law, my wife, my step-daughters and my son, my mother, my father (the father who raised and loved and supported me as I wobbled and wandered until I found a piece of property on which to set my desk), my father (the father who encoded a string of genes for me then disappeared into a myth of hardware and faith). Was Father Adam there, too? The banished Lilith? The beloved, the scorned Eve? I never eat alone.

I was whatever lie I needed to be to make the neediest other person at the table happy. The others took turns at being the neediest. I was the story I imagined each one needed to hear to feel loved. They were probably the same for me. I ordered. I ordered too much food because when I'm with family I'm afraid of going hungry.

I wanted to look her in the eye, my mother-in-law, to see if I could see who she is when all the stories about her have been stripped away. Stories I've been told over the years; stories I've added a twist to or exaggerated or composed on my own. But I didn't dare look her in the eye. I don't look anyone in the eye. I don't want you to see who, beyond the stories, I am: a liar.

I lied. I wasn't there, I didn't have dinner at that restaurant that night.

But the Oolong Chilean Sea Bass, tea marinated and broiled in sweet ginger soy, served over warm spinach, was delicious. Good boy that I am, I cleaned my plate. She treated. She added the tip and signed the slip. I helped her into the car. She was happy but for one regret, the unfinished Appletini that the server wouldn't let her take, in a plastic cup, home. I helped her out of the car, walked her to her door, kissed her goodnight, goodbye, see you again soon. I'm telling you the truth.

For Love

The book.

I left it in Jerusalem.

After 38 months in Israel, I was returning home. You were there—South Jersey. Married now. Even after three years away, I was still traumatized by first adult love. In Israel, I'd met other travelers who reported traveling for the same reason: to flee from a devastating break-up. That wasn't the only reason I traveled to Israel and stayed so long. But it was on my short list.

For love—I would

split open your head and put

a candle in

behind the eyes.

I remember the end more than the beginning, the pain more than the pleasure: the kitchen knife I threatened you with.

I remember pushing you out of a car crawling on a dark road in Medford. To frighten you even more, I drove away—but not out of sight—before I stopped to let you back into the car for the drive home.

Danny-Aldo-Jeff-Jeff-Tom—

the forms of men

you studied then.

(When I heard you'd slept with x,/I snuck into your house, ripped the dress/I bought for you hoping to ex-/tend love.)

The long, torturous period of our breaking up: when I look back on it now, it seems like it took at least half if not more of the three years we were together.

Love is dead in us

if we forget

I remember "The Rain": "All night the sound had/come back again,/and again falls/this quiet, persistent rain." In college, I wrote a paper on it. At twenty, what did I know about poetry: how to read it; how it read me.

Before "The Rain".

One summer—our first?—

at a motor lodge pool

(your uncle was the manager?)

inspired by body and what you made

happen in it, charged

with the power of sex,

I put words together.

Such a woman, such poetry:

I wanted to marry

Then in a bathtub, you said, *do you even know where it is. Touch it!* But I fumbled.

You knew

your way around

pleasure and expected me

to, too.

Was there time between the beginning and the end?

. . . love also

becomes a reward so

remote from me . . .

Lonely, mystical, horny in Safed and Jerusalem. One night in Beit HaKerem, a neighborhood in Jerusalem, a Belgian girl blew me. In Safed, an American woman who had come to Israel, after a few years in Morocco, to change her life, but I persuaded her to live immodestly for another few hours.

I was a talking wound. A sensitive mess.

I knew how to get her to undress.

I didn't know your current address.

In Israel, thousands of years came to me. I walked the walls around the Old City. I visited the tombs of prophets and kings. I was drawn into the vortex of longing-grief: thousands of pious men at the Western Wall on the night of destruction, *Tisha B'Av*, the Ninth of *Av*, when baseless hatred brought the Temple down. A rabbi wrote the story of the generations that led to me: assimilated, middle class, broken-hearted, American, Reform Jew. The link to one story broken—you and me—a link to another—Jew to history—forged.

We fucked and fought. That's what I remember. I was unlovable.

"I also have painful memories, of which I still feel very bad and guilty about. I suppose the worst one was being in the pool with J. B.... I have no idea what I was thinking... I just remember your devastated reaction (and rightly so) and me wondering what the f was I thinking... in my own way I felt a lot worse than you and that still exists."

am I to be locked in this

final uneasiness

Take a good look out the window. Take the land in. You won't be seeing it again for a long time. Whose voice? Who knew as the plane lifted off from Ben Gurion Airport? The night before, I couldn't sleep. I walked with a friend, a woman, from my apartment on Tchernichovsky Street in West Jerusalem to the Wall to pray before my early morning departure. I remember walking back through the neighborhoods, the lights all out, the sleepers' dreams floating from the beds into the streets down which I walked back home to catch the taxi that would take me away. Having left Jerusalem many times before—short trips around the country for work or pleasure—I knew what happens. When one returns, even after only a day away, she withholds. A lover betrayed. She shows you only this: a dirty, crowded city. But stay with her for a few days, she yields, she opens, she reveals. I wouldn't be returning. *For Love.*

Let me stumble into

not the confession but

the obsession I begin with

now. For you

The night I moved out of our Collingswood apartment. It was raining. Bob helped carry the furniture to the truck. You watched from your couch. Later, there were probably beers. And Bob declaiming poetry.

He lived with mice in an old farmhouse, the one you married. You'd been on and off with him throughout our time. Then, three sons later, divorced. When I heard the news, I thought: this time, this time . . .

Sunday night, some thirty years later, "this quiet, persistent rain." We risk remembering. This:

"I remember working with you

at Steak and Brew

and one night I waited

for you at some bar.

While I was waiting lots of creepy

old men were in there, slurping me. I was so happy

when you walked in, so young, so cute.

You smelled like food.

You had your sleeves rolled up."

Your memory

rewrites me.

Into the company of love

it all returns

. . . wet

with a decent happiness

Across a sea, I carried Creeley

but the book is gone

and there have been wars, theirs and ours, yours and mine

for love

Make It Old: A Wedding Anniversary Epithalamion

1.

In the beginning was a wedding.

The ceremony began with light. The ceremony included the separation of water from water, and it included the formation of land followed by the breaking apart of continents. The sound was terrible, and it was heard beyond the sky and in the perfect garden, the venue chosen for the wedding ceremony and reception.

The ceremony began before there was a brain, a human brain, before there were two human brains, even before there was a serpent brain. But there was an alphabet, and there was intelligence, and intelligence arranged the letters to form a world.

(Even now, some nights you can see in the bride's eye signs that deep inside her letters are still moving, touching, deciding to marry or drift apart: m-a-r-r-i-a-g-e, m-i-r-a-g-e, r-a-g-e, a-g-e . . .)

Crawling and swarming, the guests arrived in search of their names. The guests circled in water; the guests fluttered, leaves of trees that turned into wings of songbirds and birds of prey.

Then, after every goodness but before the creation of rest, the penultimate act of creation: groom, bride.

Thus, the ceremony unfolded.

God designed it that way. God, whose DNA were all over the linen light and in the water, in fruit and grasses, so that a forensic detective, later, would have no trouble identifying the judge who sentenced groom and bride to imprisonment in Eden, then tossed them, with hardly enough clothing to cover them and not a dime in their pockets, into the unforgiving, free world. Henceforth, every woman and man, clinging to each other, trudge away from Eden.

But created of Eden's soil and bone, what did they know about it, exile, the first bride and groom? They *created* it! In Eden, birthplace of blame. He blamed her. She blamed it. And who did God blame? Did God blame god's self for ignoring the counsel of angels who advised against creating woman and man?

Exile: where marriage truly begins.

2.

Deep in the night before *your* wedding, a howl frightened you. It has its own door, the animal, a rubber flap that swings open and slaps shut after the dog steps through. The animal goes and comes as it pleases. Heading into the woods beyond its house. Bears in those woods, coyotes.

The night before the wedding, a howl wrenched you, you and your beloved, from bed, but it was too dark to enter the woods, and maybe it was pointless, the pet already dead, so what could you do? Terrified, you pulled up two chairs and, facing each other, you and your beloved, you began to sing *The Song of Songs* to each other. The book said that was a tradition.

"Oh, give me of the kisses of your mouth,
For your love is more delightful than wine.
Your ointments yield a sweet fragrance,
Your name is like finest oil—
Therefore maidens love you.
Draw me after you, let us run!"

(Is the dog alive?)

"You have captured my heart,
My own, my bride,
You have captured my heart
With one glance of your eyes,
With one coil of your necklace.
How sweet is your love,
My own, my bride!

How much more delightful your love than wine,
Your ointments more fragrant
Than any spice!"

(Did you hear that, that bellow?)

The Song of Songs: the first bride, the first groom, for them it was a song without a dog. Love was created before male and female they were crafted. Before life into them was blown, this song.

Because you are contrary, because you came to life and lost your hair too soon in the Age of Aquarius, you refused the laws of assimilation and embraced the manual of tradition, *The New Jewish Wedding Book*, a book for a generation of Jews whose motto is *make it old.*

Thus, the *kittel*, the wedding gown/burial shroud you donned; thus the *ketubah*, the signing, in the presence of witnesses, the marriage contract; thus the *bedeken*, the veiling by the groom of the bride; thus the *huppah*, the wedding canopy, and the *sheva brachot,* seven blessings, and *yihud,* the moments of privacy, immediately following the ceremony, a guard outside the door, for the newlyweds to sip each other's wine; thus the *badhen*, the jester at the reception. And for your guests, citizens of United Secular America: a program to explain the strange performance.

You and your bride, born into the long shadow of Eden, born into love sung by ancestors, born into the sound of tumbling Temple stones translated into broken glass echoing all the way from 70 CE Jerusalem to 1933 Berlin, from early twentieth-century New York to late twentieth-century Asheville.

You added the sound of your own shattered glass to the soundtrack of your people.

Breaking the glass: a moment followed by a kiss, a cheer, a song: *siman tov u'mazal tov,* good sign and good luck.

Breaking the *self,* your precious, single, defended and reinforced-for-decades (you married at 36) self: the steady work of marriage.

Twenty-five years now. Beautiful bride, wise wife, and shards to show for love, for life.

The *Huppah*

In the sixth or seventh year
of their marriage, the *huppah*
was stolen. It had absorbed
the love that was consecrated
under it, or it had absorbed nothing
and was merely fabric zipped
into a bag and of no value
to the thief, or it was a thin
blanket to cover his little girl
on an autumn night, or it was a wrap
with a rainbow of stripes
knotted around his woman
before and after a good fuck.

Of no use to a guy looking
for a quick fix of his broken life,
it may have been tossed into bushes
outside a church or into a dumpster.

The *huppah* had no mouth
to sing the bride's song,
here I am, take me home.
It had no money to pay
for space in a closet or a drawer
in some row-house. Though it looked
like it could have belonged to a magic
act, it knew no tricks, it could not assist
in sleight-of-hand. Though it looked
sacred, it could not purify human flesh.

It's been a dozen years
since the *huppah* was taken from them,
since it went out into a city of mustard
and minute steak, of a cracked bell and hall
of freedom, and whether it was hauled
to a landfill with all the other refuse

of a fat city, or tacked to a wall and draped
over a window to keep a brother, a cop
from stealing a look at a brother's girl
moving toward him with all that's good
to eat, or whether it was offered
to an oil drum's angry fire
around which six day laborers gather
waiting for the dock to open—
it's all the same to them. The mortgage

is hungry and must be fed. The children
are stupid and must be prodded
toward the pen where they will be civilized
and milked. The marriage is short
on memory and must be consecrated
again and again, with a glance that shoots
from bride to groom, groom to bride
under the *huppah* of sky
that fills with clouds and empties, that trembles
dark and light, that must be held in place
by some angels, maybe the same angels
that held their original *huppah*
for the brief ceremony that preceded
the long ordeal and party of love.

Mezuzah

Tell all the truth but—
Emily Dickinson

You shall love . . .
Deuteronomy 6:5

Mezuzah: a small, rectangular case containing verses from
Torah affixed aslant to the doorpost of one's house

For each of
the moods of

marriage the small
lies that keep

our lives whole
as we cross

the threshold, passing
the commandment to

love nailed slant
to the doorpost

II. The Book of Brothers

from *The Book of Brothers*

In Rebekah's womb
two maps are drawn, and you thought
she gave birth to boys.

*

As far as their aching
for freedom can see, it's Rebekah's womb
all the way to the horizon.

*

Delivery: Jacob reaches
for Esau's heel.

Sun and shadow
face the desert rocks.

*

Night. Esau plays
with his brother. Jacob's lying
on hard ground, but everything's standing
up inside him. Full moon.

*

What god would be attracted
to him, Esau wonders as he touches
his brother's hairless chest.

*

Esau's hairy chest—
in Lithuania, rabbis caress
each verse. Foreplay.

The moon waxing over the forest
where they will be shot.

*

Nothing smells worse
than goat hair, says Rashi.

Garlic pickle paradise in the barrel
on the street below the open window
of the study hall.

*

Night. In the tent
Esau makes the sound of a wolf.
Jacob tastes hunter's flesh.

*

Night. Side by side.
In the tent, Jacob and Esau
ejaculate. Shooting stars.

*

Trades
his birthright for lentils
in the belly: Esau.

*

Beautiful then gone:
Jacob's twilit face, Esau's
spoon of beans.

*

In father's blind eye, a wild
animal bound for slaughter—
Esau in the field.

*

Isaac's blind—or nearly so—
This makes the rabbis crazy—
One *midrash* competes with another
in a room lit only by ink.

*

Esau's bow, god's arrow—
it brings the hunted
to its knees then to fire—
Isaac smells love, night.

*

Such an old man—
tent flap closed at noon, vulture
drawing zeroes in the sky.

*

Isaac doesn't know
he's going to die:
Rebekah's moonlit face.

*

Old Isaac doesn't
know he's going to die:
he smells wet cattle.

*

"Going to die"—at noon
the shadow draws in, hides
in the rock.

Rabbi spits
an olive pit into his hand.

*

Rain touches his eye
and the hairy hand
he holds in his hands:
Isaac's blessing.

*

A stone takes off
from a cliff, a bird.
Mother betrayed him: Esau.

*

Among storehouses
of grain, brimming cisterns
and cattle, Esau
broken by the wrong
blessing that whispers to him
all night from the stone-pillow.

*

"A vacant man" says Rashi—
How many rabbis
study Esau's meaninglessness
well past midnight?

*

Winter
touches these brothers, hundreds
of miles apart.

*

Even after the angel
names him Israel, Jacob
reaches for Esau's heel.

His Murderer *and* His Keeper

Some days I can't remember: am I Abel or Cain?

Once, I was a shepherd. Now I am reduced to this: a symbol. My brother discovered his black heart when he heard me in the field, singing, offering the best of my flock. God loves my poetry. In response, brother stoned me. Because back then no one knew when the soul leaves the body, he pummeled me beyond necessity. Even to this hour he continues, pelting me with rubble, rockets—whatever's at hand. An innocent man, dead. I must be Abel.

Useless, he lies forever in a field while I wander, village to village, continent to continent, transferring my power from nation to nation, one century after another. No one can touch me. I am indestructible! But powerless: I cannot die.

One summer day, I was playing on the beach with three other boys, cousins. Behind us, our city was burning. Before us, the sea was a wide, knowing eye, its gaze fixed on the merciful sky. Suddenly, a message was delivered to my cousins and me. It came from overhead, it arrived, and we were mist but famous in newspapers around the world. Not even God's mercy is safe when Cain governs the sky.

For breakfast, eggs. For lunch, bitterness: my co-worker's promotion over me. For supper, envy: my neighbor's voluptuous wife. Call me Cain.

There is a hole for people like him, murderers, a cell with an eye-level slit in the door through which to see a slice of world. But somehow he multiplies in the free world while I, alone, the weight of the whole earth on my chest, wait forever to adjust to the imprisoning dark.

Am I Cain when I terminate the pregnancy? Am I Abel when I love the soon-to-be born who, whether they come broken or whole, will be delivered from Father to Son who will love and forgive them the sin of life?

Cain and Abel: Am I a brother? Cain or Abel: Am I an only child, the salvageable part of a wrecked marriage, the issue of a mistake caught and corrected?

I hear how he tends to aging father, anxious mother, repaying the impossible debt of his reckless youth, desperate to make amends. Installing a chandelier so that in their new apartment there will be light—is this how Cain becomes Abel?

It was his blood on the sheet where holy love tossed for an hour when she first surrendered to my charm decades ago. This morning, it's his blood that congeals on the nick in my shaved neck. It doesn't cry out to me, his blood. It doesn't speak at all, but it stains and it salts and it puddles and pools and there's nowhere I can turn to escape it. It's in the silver tines of the fork as well as the stabbed meat; it's in the Rembrandt, the Rothko, and the Modigliani: there is nowhere where I am not his murderer, his keeper.

Praise. Praise his fortitude. Crossing a border or a century, cleaning a weapon or clearing a heart: he meets every threat with poise, and he endures. I can't keep from praising him. It's the only defense I have, praising brother who helped me develop a taste for my own sweet blood.

In the middle of eternal exile, somewhere in downtown America, I lift my eyes: where is my refuge, where my home? In a field bloody with spring flowers, I lower my eyes to fertile soil from where my help, o brother, may come.

Cain and Abel: it's just a story, right? There never were two brothers, one a Christian, the other a Jew; one a body, the other a soul. One man. One man with two or 102 responses to the punishment, the gift of life.

The Book of Brothers

Reading it, *The Book of Brothers*, the sisters
are by turns amused, appalled, and bored.
Those boys, they think.

To read about themselves, the sisters
should listen to the turning page of the sea, should turn
to the page of menstrual blood. Their darkness

knows how life pushes through to light.
But the sisters are taught to read
The Good Book, the *only* book for them,

The Book of Brothers. And what
is its first letter, its first lesson?
Bet. The letter for *bayit.* House.

See, they are told, this is your house,
make it home, a home for your brothers
and you. The sisters understand.

Until *The Book of Sisters* is discovered,
the sisters read but resist
The Book of Brothers. Their lives

are Torah, too, but told
in a holy language
boys will never wholly understand.

III. Re: Writing Torah

And Holy

What came before "there was evening and there was morning, a *first* day," and "there was evening and there was morning, a *second* day," and "there was evening and there was morning, a *third* day," and so on until "the heaven and earth were finished," and God "ceased on the *seventh* day from all the work that He had done," and "God blessed the *seventh* day and declared it holy"?

In other words, what came before "numbering our days," one through seven?

*

Before light, darkness.
Before light . . . Before light . . .

In darkness, I cry
into darkness and darkness
replies with darkness.

Before light, Eden and exile
are one: Darkness.

Darkness is. Then
it dissolves.
Like black aspirin in water.

Now light is. Light is silver and plum, feathered
and furrowed, light is the frosted
wave washing ashore and the particles
where sea meets land, land
meets sea, and all the way
to the horizon where day
meets day meets night meets day.

Before
light no
before

And light is
memory: there was darkness.

And light is
fear: will darkness return?

*

Again. Before
light, darkness.
In
that darkness—all there was—,
no question, no
yearning.

Then there was light. And any creatures
stunned by light, any form of
life that favored darkness, created
this: yearning.
Yearning for darkness.

And there was evening, and there was morning, and there was evening. And
those creatures that came to light in light, who favored light, yearned for light.

*

And there was evening, and there was vanishing. And there was morning, and
there was vanishing.

And there was evening, and there was morning: vanishing and vanishing.
Into this
were we born: vanishing.

And we were born into this: yearning.

Soulmates: yearning/vanishing.

No, not mates: not two souls
joined/separated
by a forward slash.

One Soul.

From Oneness
we come. To Oneness
we return.

But can we dwell, while we're here, in Oneness? While we are here.

O Israel, Y-H-V-H is
Our God, Y-H-V-H is
YearningVanishing (YV) (One) (H H).

*

What does it take to make the world
whole?

Darkness and
light.

Heaven and
Earth.

Vanishing and
yearning.

Work and
rest.

And and *And.*

And: creator
of the holy

One.

The Way of Gods and Women

. . . but why did you steal my gods?
Laban to Jacob
GEN 31:30

. . . anyone with whom you find your gods shall not remain alive!
Jacob to Laban
GEN 31:32

If, from afar, they saw
her kiss him at the well
they did not say.

Nor did they murmur, her
household gods,
when she ran past them
to announce
his arrival.

When, as her sister increased,
son by son by son, each
extending Leah's future,
Rachel saw her future
wither. Her household
gods offered her nothing.

Even on the road
to Canaan, when she sat
on them and would not rise
for Laban, seeking
his stolen gods, they
stayed true
to their nature, keeping
quiet when Rachel lied
that the way of
women was upon her.

Their power
was their refusal
to give anything
more than themselves.

My Stone

Of the daily
burden of ruling
creation, what
does God know?

I am Herod.
I send the hand
of ambition
as far as sky.
No limit
to my stone.

God breathed
human life
into motion, then,
once He knew
woman and man, what
they were, He turned
away. He never
looked back.

Now only I am.
Herod, I build
on a scale beyond
betrayal.

The Rest Is Prayer

the Temple Institute, preparing to build the Third Temple in Jerusalem
–www.templeinstitute.org

Tabernacle replaced by Temple,
Temple replaced by longing for its return.

Even this evening, this very hour, thousands
bow in the direction of its absence, hundreds kiss

proximal stone, Western retaining wall.
But only a chosen few

measure the robe, shape laver and bowl,
and weigh, on the scale of sacred law, the cost

of waiting for politics to fail, the benefit
of forcing holiness.

The rest is prayer.

They rehearse psalms of the steps.
They will be ready to rise in praise,

these men with their end of days
at hand, these faithful men

next in the unbroken
line of Temple priests.

To Be Read before Reciting the Blessing for the Washing of Hands

Bite-the-hand-that-feeds-you
bites hand-that-rocks-the-cradle.

Blood-on-the-hands listens
to wash-your-hands-of-it.

The devil, to be the devil, needs
idle hands.

Its hands full of fear
of losing everything: hands-off.

Elsewhere, give-me-a-hand and lend-a-hand
accomplish more than upper-hand.

Passover: bird-in-the-hand
frees the bird.

The hour's always right to lift your hands and pray,
Let lay-a-hand-on-someone keep his hands
clean tonight.

Confession

Yom Kippur 5774

I rise with the congregation.

I form a fist. They form a fist. We form a fist. The fist is personal. The fist is communal. *We have sinned.* The fist knocks on my chest. *We have sinned.* The fist knocks on their chest. *We have sinned.* The fist knocks on our chest. The fist knocks.

I chant, they chant, we chant:

We have sinned, betrayed, robbed, and deceived.

At each sin, the fist knocks on the chest. *We have betrayed.* The fist knocks. The chest is a door. Anyone home?

We have robbed. (I didn't rob. I think I didn't rob. Did I steal someone's good name?) The fist taps on the chest.

We have deceived. (I can't remember; did I deceive anyone this year?)The fist strikes the chest *for the sin we committed by forgetting our sins.*

The fist strikes. Is the heart at home? Is any heart at home? What *does* the heart remember, what insult does it still smart from, what insult did it deliver?

To the right of me, my wife. She remembers. She knows which of the transgressions are mine. *We have acted stubbornly*. Our fists knock, my wife's fist and my fist. Is she confessing for my stubbornness? Is my stubbornness her stubbornness? Our fist knocks.

We have acted maliciously (the fist knocks), *violently* (the fist knocks). Violently? Was I among the masked settlers who set fire to a tool shed in the village, the shed used to store tools for building a water reservoir to serve a few villages in the West Bank?

The settlers: are they my people? Are we one, the settlers and me? My heart hardens.

I think of the rockets and rhetoric hurled, this year as in years past—*Zionism is a germ of corruption that will be wiped off the face of the earth*—and my heart hardens. My fist knocks.

We have led others astray. Is that what I have done this year by inviting into my house, our house, *The Gatekeepers* and *Five Broken Cameras,* films troubled by the occupation, concerned about the policies and practices of the state, the State of Israel, the land in which I experienced, decades ago, my Jewish awakening, where I felt more at home than I have ever felt anywhere else? The fist knocks.

I look up from my confession. A few rows in front of me, closer to the ark, closer to the Torah, a congregant whose views on Israel I think I know. In his eyes, am I trouble, am I traitor? I see him. My heart hardens. Does his heart harden when he sees me? *We have been obstinate*. Our fists knock.

I look up from my confession, and I look around the congregation. There the lay leaders, so dedicated, so true to *halakhah*, Jewish law, and there the worshippers who faithfully attend services, Shabbat after Shabbat after Shabbat. And I look at those who create and participate in community life, potlucks, rummage sales, concerts, Israel's Independence Day.

I pay my dues, I participate when it's convenient, I offer a *d'var Torah*, a talk on the Torah portion of the week, twice a year, I chant *haftarah*, a reading from prophets, two or three times a year. Mostly, however, I hover on the margins of the community. Where am I now, as I stand among the worshippers, eight or nine rows back from the front of the sanctuary, in the middle of the row?

If the community were to turn to me now and call my name, *Ya'akov* (my Hebrew name), would I respond like Abraham, when God calls his name, *Hineini,* Here am I? I am here, not merely among or with you but *of* you. Could I say this without it being a lie? *We spread lies.*

The fist knocks, the fist knocks, the fist knocks.

What's this? Do I sense that deep inside my chest the heart stirs? Or am I the child knocking, desperately knocking on mother's locked bedroom door, the television blaring "Days of Our Lives," mother passed out on the bed?

Oh Mother Oh God Oh God Oh Mother, what have I done, what have we done (*we have acted perversely*), please open the door, please receive me, receive us, that we may confess to what we know and what we know not (*we have given bad advice, we have committed abominations*), and please, please God/Mother/Father/King forgive us!

I stand with the congregation. On the margin, among. I am as steady on my feet and as unsteady as my fellow congregants. Those I know well, those I hardly know, those I respect, those I scorn, and those who I fear look at me skeptically—High Holiday Jew, meditating Jew, poet, liberal, infrequent presence in this Conservative *beit tefillah*, house of prayer.

Here we are, each in the privacy of his and her own book of life, in which we've recorded, committed, each in his or her own breath and blood, the sentences of our actions, thoughts, and feelings over the last year (*we have transgressed*), terribly alone, terribly together, confessing and beating, beating, beating our heart, our stubborn, collective heart into submission, into awareness, into life.

Enemies of Israel, Enemies of the Jews

The enemy of Israel shakes hands with the enemy of the Jews. The mother of the kidnapped scholar shakes. An explosion; five fresh eggs shake.

In some places, the enemies of the Jews disguise themselves as enemies of Israel. In some places, an enemy of Israel disguises himself as a Jew, a Hasid in fedora boarding an Egged bus.

Some days, the enemies of Israel and the enemies of the Jews quietly sip coffee. Yesterday, a sliver of quiet while the mob on the Parisian street caught its breath.

You going to the Enemies of the Jews show? The Enemies of Israel is opening.
Nah. I hate heavy metal.

An enemy of Israel marries an enemy of the Jews. Their daughter, a religious Zionist, marries a boy in the elite, IDF Givati Brigade.

Come, says god, at the start of each new day. *Come*, says god, to the enemy of the Jews, *be part of my creation*.

The enemies of the Jews cheer when the enemies of Israel have their day. But their cheer turns to anger when a Jew pops up alive here and there, on CNN, in the *Jew York Times*.

Like Israel, the enemies of Israel dream of peace.

I'm an American Jew, but sometimes it seems that I, too, live within the borders of Israel, greater Israel. Is that how you see me, enemy of Israel? Or do you see me as an old-fashioned cosmopolitan Jew?

After fighting ends, the enemies of Israel gather remains of dead houses, donkeys, sons. Around the world, enemies of the Jews grumble, mutter, vow not to rest as long as there is a Jew somewhere in the world who prays, "You have not granted this day, Shabbat, Lord our God, to other peoples of the world."

At the South Carolina beach in August, the tide is high then low, high then low. Are any of the vacationers on Edisto Island enemies of Israel or enemies of the

Jews? Yes? No? Judging only by their skimpy and modest bathing suits, their splendid, bulging, or sagging flesh, it's hard to know.

The enemies of Israel, enemies of the Jews: journalists? architects? engineers? Bankers, barbers, athletes, clerks? Look around the room. There's room enough for everyone to join the party, room enough even for a stray Israeli, a deluded Jew. ("Some of us," says one congregational rabbi, "are our own worst enemies.")

The enemies of Israel are growing impatient, while the enemies of the eternal Jews bide their time. The enemies of the Jews know better than you how hard it is to rid the world, as god has commanded them, of Jews.

Even when Israel recedes, for a period, from the news, the enemies of Israel continue to gather material for the day when Israel will explode again in print and on screens around the world.

The friends of Israel? I will get to them another day.

And what of the famous wolf, the famous lamb? They are weary, they would like to lie, already, side by side, on the grass. Some days the enemies of Israel and Israel are weary, too. So, they agree to a fragile, fraught, fierce truce, and lie, each in their place, suspicious neighbors in a somewhat long and narrow land.

I have placed before you, said god to the ancient Israelites, *a curse and a curse. Secure a path between them.* So they tried, in ancient times, and try today.

Those who kill our children must be killed. Who said this, the enemies of Israel or Israelis, the enemies of the Jews or Jews?

It's unlikely that Jerusalem will be destroyed, but who knows? It's happened before. Before the Iron Dome. Before the Dome of the Rock.

So many Jews, so many kinds of Jews gather in all-purpose rooms all across America to support Israel and learn a thing or two about its latest war. What unites is what divides them: a speaker's characterization of the enemies of Israel and the superiority of Jews. Meanwhile, the enemies of Israel, the enemies of the Jews seek a cure for modernity.

The enemies of the Jews love the Jew, their creator without whom they would not exist. The enemies of Israel love Israel, which, after all, they helped create.

If there's a solution to the problem of Israel and its enemies, it's unlikely to come from a U.N. resolution.

For some, the hour is late. What do they hear as they lie in bed awake all night? The chink, chink of the digging of tunnels? The whistle of rockets? The hum of drones? Will better angels ever return to a broken, divided land? To whom will they speak? What will they say? For now, at night, some pray, some tremble, some weep.

How god Came to Be God

Now I know how god came to be God. There was a father. (Could it have been a mother?) There was a son. (Could it have been a daughter?)The father knew what his days were, his nights. For as long as there was a son in his life, he knew what his days and nights were.

His son took steps, his son absorbed language. Thoughts came to the boy, feelings came. And he began to express himself. Body language. Speech.

There was food and the boy savored some dishes, pushed others away. One day the boy turned and he favored those he had previously despised, despised those he had once enjoyed.

There were other people around. The father saw how they responded to his son. The boy's gifts: intelligence and charm. The father welcomed their kind words about his son. Lowering his eyes, he received their praise.

There were other fathers with sons and daughters, and those boys and girls came to his son and left his son. There was a room in which they lay around waiting for the invention of sex.

Beyond the room, there were obstacles and the boy was bruised. Bruised, he returned to the room. Not yet healed, he left the room and stayed away a little longer and a little longer each season.

There was an hour when the son would leave for an entire season and another season. They had prepared for this hour, prepared in many ways. There was conversation, there was money, there was education, there was sport . . .

There was a calendar, and the minute of the son's departure was marked on the calendar. (This was before planners, before Google calendar. I don't know how appointments were recorded back then, and I don't care. This isn't history. This isn't archeology. This isn't anthropology. This is fable. This is truth.)

Where the son would go at the appointed hour was known. There was a universe, and the son's access to the universe and his purpose in it passed through a university, which would exist, for the boy, for four years, maybe a little longer, before it vanished, leaving the boy standing in a city of doors and mysterious faces.

(In the Torah, there is no before, no after. Abraham observed the laws of *kashrut*, the dietary laws, even before they were given. Moses sat in the *beit midrash*, the rabbinic study hall, listening to a lesson being taught by Rabbi Akiva who lived many generations after Moses. Here, too, in this world of my making, the laws of linear time are suspended. Thus, before god creates humans, before god is God, she studies at the university the ways of all beings and gods. Then comes law. Then comes love.)

The father could see, as it approached, the hour of parting, the hour when he would become something new (he knew not what) or nothing. Aware of his son's, his only son's imminent departure, he sensed that a world was about to be withdrawn from him.

Once there was not god. There was just parent and child, father and son. For a time there was an illusion of their being one.

Then there was parting, there was separation and distance, boundless absence.

Call it, this boundlessness, this absence, the father thought, call it . . . but his body made no sound.

God couldn't help him then, God who knows the price of delivering Her own daughters and sons to the world, and loving them even as they grow away from Her, as they must, and calling this *good.*

are you my god

> *in every generation, each person must regard himself or herself as if he or she were the one liberated, on the very night of Passover, from Egypt*
> –adapted from the Passover Haggadah

This won't do, the *seder*
your grandmother cooked
and indexed on
cards to leap down
the generations;
this won't
do, the *seder* sanctioned
by the rabbi, four
cups and mortar-board bread.
No! Your religious
uncle's orderly
seder won't do!
Your *seder* must light
the fuse that will ignite
the bomb that will free
the suburban
house of its roof, blasting it
open to stars and moon,
sending you like a letter
of a holy alphabet blown
apart into the night
to roam with dogs, to drink
the soiled birdbath water
in some mayor's yard, to
scream like a burning
refugee, and knock
on door and door and door
asking *is this*
my home and
will you let me
eat and *are you*
my god, my god

Re: Writing Torah

on Shavuot, the Jewish holiday celebrating the giving of Torah

Before there was screen there was paper; before paper, papyrus; before papyrus, stone.

What happened at Sinai?

O God and Moses
Poet and Muse

Whatever happened at Sinai, there was a story about words inscribed on stone and the stone in the story, the stone with words inscribed on it, was smashed, the words shattered, the blood and bones of the words scattered and spilled, impossible to reconstruct.

O Moses and God
Poet and Muse

Whatever happened at Sinai, there were some words shattered and some words uttered again, and there was a second stone with words.

O Vision, O Holy
Re-Vision

Whatever happened at Sinai eventually was a story inscribed on goatskin about words inscribed on stone—words for the people to follow all the way to the world's redemption.

O restless, we search
the words for wisdom
and peace, and we compose
ourselves—our history, our fantasy—
with words of Torah and how we know
when they aren't quite
right, the words we choose,

we don't know, we can't say,
and deleting takes
as much audacity as smashing,
and the blank screen
is as unforgiving as the blank tablet,
and we could turn
away from the test, the task,
we could live
but we are not free, Torah says,
to receive Torah as it is.
Torah requires resistance, revision.
Maybe then
in the light of
what's rewritten
our life will become
light in
which our children
and theirs will see
life.

IV. What I've Been Given

Dear Time

I can't get away from you.

You are strapped to my wrist. You are in my pocket. You quietly command the corner of the screen, you are broadcast on every station, you are . . .

A constant reminder: I'm almost out of you. I must hurry to finish . . . What if I run out of you (or is it the other way around, what if you run out of me?) before I finish . . . finish what? This sentence? This life?

You are a problem. Are you *the* problem?

What shall I call you?

What shall I call you who never respond to my sighs, my pleas?

Father Time.

But you go by a hundred names: Game Time, Show Time, Face Time, Down Time, Overtime, Outta Time,
Hard Time, Air Time, Party Time, Closing Time . . .

You entered my life at conception. Since then, I've lost people, places, and things—Uncle Al, Cousin Connie, my tickets to the original Woodstock, my hair—but I haven't lost you, haven't been able to shake you, and you haven't yet ditched me.

I am still learning, decades on and still learning how to be son, brother, husband, father, colleague, congregant, friend. And how to live with you, my assassin.

As if to defeat you, I've stuffed more activities into my minutes, my hours, my days and nights than I believed they could contain, and I've taken a Sabbath sip, now and then, of eternity.

Still you abide with me.

Though we are, for now, inseparable, the time will come when we, you and I, Dear Time, will part. Until then, consider me yours. In exchange for my loyalty to you, I'm counting on you to be true to me until the end of time. My dear time.

Hide and Seek

Let the words find you, you who have been hiding from them for so long.

Which words?

The words carried by the river whose source is unknown—unknown, though many have sought it.

The river's source may be hidden, but I am not. I am right here. Listening to a voice whine about illness, deadlines, divorce. Her words find me shaving, showering, dressing for a cold day. Are these the words?

Fresh Air. Listening to a podcast of yesterday's interview while you prepare for this day is one way to hide.

I hide from people, not voices, not books.

You hide in the voices of others.

Who are you?

I know your father, both of your fathers, Pharaoh and Joseph. I know your birth father, the one who spoke once before your memory was born and then was never heard from again, and I know your life father, the one who gave you a roof, an education, a nation in (from) which to hide.

A nation, an unbreachable wall.

It will be breached, just like the walls that secured your temple, the walls that enclosed the empty holiness of holiness.

Who are you?

I am unpublished, unsanctified, unborn. I meet none of your criteria for authority. Yet, I call you forth and you respond. I hold your attention.

You say, I say.
When I would sit at ease,
comes word to word to word—
an infectious disease.

Or sanctuary: the book of praise, the book of pleas.

I know the book of pleas, I know the book of praise, pages I turn and turn but the prayer book's too heavy to take flight, its thousand wings do not suffice to lift it though occasionally a word darts from the page to

your heart.

How did you find me?

I never lost you. I have been with you all along.

Who are you?

I am the Word of words, Voice of voices.

You hide in others' voices?

Live, not hide. If not in others' voices, how could you hear me?

Are you dead or alive?

Alive. I live. As long as you can hear me, I live.
I speak to but I cannot speak
for you.

How can I speak of my encounter with you in a way that others will believe me?

Let the words find you, you who have been hiding from them for so long.

The Poems Left In Me

with gratitude to the poets whose poems gave me this

The poems left in me five summers and five long winters, boatloads of thuya, silence on a peak in Darien, and a room in which every suffering has a different smell.

The poems left in me grass all blowing in the same direction, twenty-seven bathers and one woman, one yearning woman, watching from behind curtains, and angel-headed hipsters on negro streets at dawn searching for an angry fix.

The poems slipped into me, though not like an intruder. The poems left, when I turned the page, when I shelved the wafer-thin book, when I darkened the screen, leaving behind a still, unravished bride. The poems left with a bow not knowing to what.

I would like to say the poems create the eye through which they enter, the ear with which I hear them. I would like to say that the poems form neural pathways in the brain, pathways, in my case, well worn and maintained, regularly tended and groomed. I would like to say that the photons of a poem illuminate my body from within.

I would like to say that I welcome each poem equally—the awful rowing of this one, the hammer of that one swinging overhead so strong, overhead so sure—the way Abraham welcomes strangers to his tent: with lamb, with warmth. They are angels, but Abraham discovers this only after they have gone, only after the miracle they promised comes true.

The poems promised me nothing. More than traces, more than wisps, the poems left in me paired butterflies and squealing housewives. They left in me god's wrath, coiled forever in my questioning. They left in me a drunk sailor dreaming of baboons.

A door closing on a room to which men at forty will never return, bare-ruined choirs where late the sweet birds sang, a church inside which nothing is going on, a filling station, its oil cans arranged to say so, so, so . . .

Where was it one first heard the truth? The *the*.

A collector's life, though what I've collected is rarely on display.

Do not be deceived by the shelves and stacks of books in my office, throughout my home. If you think they are what I hold dear, go ahead, choose one and slip it from the shelf, lift it from the stack. Every word in its place. Not a word, phrase, line, stanza missing. No evidence of what the poems left in me.

My annotations? They prove nothing, neither that this poem left lions in me nor that the other poem left in me a cup with a chipped lip.

Downward to darkness on extended wings: a private life.

So private even I don't know why it chooses this line rather than that, why it chooses to release, when it does, this line in particular to resound in brain and heart.

Ah, the heart, the forgotten dialect of it, music that hurts.

Where the dearest freshness lives: deep down.

Put your ear to my chest. Can you hear the mermaids, America singing its letter of recommendation? Now, in the black milk of daybreak, seems it rich . . . sorry I cannot travel the endless distance . . . longing . . . tolls me back . . .

The poems left in me a queer gathering, a mother skunk, a fork, a flight of small schools and creeds that must have crept right out of hell, a thirst for salt. And when I could not see to see, when the last book was flung, mother finally ******, when I dipped my spoon into the alphabet soup of time, when the chicken hawk flew overhead on its way home, when the tourist from Syracuse stared back at me in the men's room mirror, I alone in the fluorescent moment of recognition knew that I have never been alone.

Michiko, Kai, and Carl, pale Ramón, stout Cortez, Richard Cory, Shulamith, Robert Boardman Vaughan: the poems left in me your names. In memory, my memory, they live. From memory, they are retrieved.

As long as words, what the poems left in me, survive, they may be retrieved again, recovered.

Fragments: keep me whole.

Remembered, misremembered: as freezing persons recollect the snow, first—chill—then stupor—then—letting go.

What I've Been Given

Six dogs: Snoopy, Prince, Woody, Ramona, Leon, Bubby. All but Bubby (mostly lab, with maybe a little Rhodesian Ridgeback, and maybe a little Golden Retriever mixed in) now nothing more than names.

Apology: not in the old high sense (think Sidney's "Apology for Poetry"). Rather, this: *Let me introduce myself: I'm sorry-that-I-didn't-visit-you-in-the-hospital; I'm sorry-that-I-haven't-called-you-in-a-year; I'm sorry-that-I'm-not-as-good-a-storyteller-as-you; I'm sorry-I-haven't-read-that-classic-book; I'm sorry-that-I'm-not-as-smart-as-you; I'm sorry-that-these-books-my-gift-to-you-contain-only-mediocore-poems-my-poems; I'm sorry-that-I've-spoken-when-I-should-have-just-listened . . . Nice to meet you.*

Proof: the books on my desk, the books to the right of me in the bookcase beside the window that looks out on a little piece of undeveloped woods, the books behind me, four bookcases full, lining the entire wall on the other side of which is our bedroom, with its own bookshelf: *The Torah: A Woman's Commentary*; *Everything Is God*; *Insight Meditation*; *Sabbatai Sevi: the Mystical Messiah*; *Proust and the Squid: The Story and Science of the Reading Brain*; Zukofsky's *A*. Thousands of unread pages. Proof of my fear of death: every title added to the stack by my desperate attempt to guarantee the future, my future: time to read.

Talent: one friend's a singer of sacred music; one friend translates the music of one tongue into the music of another; one friend cures me when he can, and, when he cannot, he steers me down the hall, from door to door, one specialist to the next, and turns me over to their care. These are my talents, my friends.

Coasts: Malibu to Margate. Malibu was yesterday, yes, yesterday, a trail in Solstice Canyon; a pier, sea-air, a long view of cliffs and coastline swinging out to sea: the beauty of what can be beheld but not be held, sealed in the specimen jar called memory, its beauty preserved to cheer me when I'm in need of cheering. Margate was ages ago, a childhood, a wave, a milkshake, a Jitney ride away from the roasted air of Planter's Peanuts on the boardwalk. These are my coordinates, given to me by divorce, which also gave me distance, which I cherish and hold, which is why I hug the edges of a continent.

Time: this day, for instance. Risen from fitful sleep into a plan to fill the open hours ahead; turned aside from the self-inflicted schedule by a phone call from a doctor, a dear friend, with word of his referral to a humble surgeon; pulled, after the first of what I'd intended to be forty minutes, off the meditation bench by the sound of a son's voice come to life earlier than I'd expected, my need to see him, to hear his plans for the day greater, I think, than his need to see me before he speeds from the house; then reset, reset the timer which will strike its bell deeper into the morning than I had intended but who's expecting evidence of my productivity today, no one, so the time's mine to use however I choose, or am I time's to use for its own inscrutable purpose? Nonetheless, time, *my* time: to read four pages of poetry, to compose two or three sentences, to slide a "mouse," drag an arrow to task bar where I click open e-mail.

Pounds: today, 155 pounds. How much does my worry weigh? How much does my fear weigh? How much does my resistance weigh? How much does my ambition weigh, my guilt, my desire, my grief, my my my my . . . ? Your love of me, and yours and yours and yours—love which I receive, love against which I protect myself, how much does that weigh? And if I were to subtract the combined weight of all this from the total? How much would I weigh then? And all the books in my house plus the books at my office—do they weigh more or less than wisdom? If I have gained, over the years, any wisdom, does it weigh enough to register on the bathroom scale?

What have I been given? This breath. This one. Mind that wanders. Will that brings it back from Los Angeles to Asheville, to Skyview Circle, to this room, this bench, back from my longing for love, your love, to the muscles of my belly, expanding, contracting. That's all.

Enough/not enough: salmon, insurance, socks, recognition, frequent flier miles, minutes, leg room, confidence, savings, patience, pens, Hebrew, education, sun block, solitude, luck . . .

Something to lose: this body.

My *kaddish*: A., M., and G., who know the prayer, the mourner's *kaddish*: *Yitgadal v'yitkadash sh'mei raba*: May God's name be exalted and hallowed . . . To them, one day, I will give the opportunity to fulfill the *mitzvah* (the commandment) of mourning the death of a parent—this gift from the same person to whom is given the awful power of hurting them with my passing.

Appointments, tickets (parking, speeding, concert), a Super 8 camera, excuses, half of my genetic history, an astrological sign (Sagittarius), stocks, uncommon health problems, students, offices, rain, sunrise seen from the top of Mt. Sinai, seat in a waiting room: I have been given these by cops, a guest at my bar mitzvah, receptionists, parents, the state of North Carolina, the laws of nature.

And, on this earth, I have been given one wife, one wise woman to oppose me, to expose the heavily guarded borders of ego, my raw need to be right, right about this, right about that, one strong woman to be buffeted by my sharp reactions to the ways another intelligent, compassionate being sees the problem (the problem that is the world, contracted now to the size of a man and a woman in a surgeon's office) and a prudent course of action. Through her, I am given the gift of the world—the whole, expansive, inclusive, imperfect world with its myriad ways of being—so long as she is not broken by my resistance to her.

When We Die

A text from a friend: "What do you believe happens when we die?"

She recently lost her son. He must have been no older than his late twenties, maybe early thirties. Over the years, she had told me enough about him to know he was troubled. I didn't really know what kind of trouble. I knew she worried about him, about his ability to take care of himself. I don't know how he died. I can only imagine.

But I cannot imagine what it feels like to have lost a son or daughter. I want to comfort my friend, but I don't know how.

I promised to respond to her question—weeks ago. I still haven't responded. I couldn't imagine how, in a text message, I could respond—the thought of thumbing all the letters necessary to offer what would inevitably be an inadequate response.

When we die: if we die on a sunny day, the sun will continue to illuminate mailbox and fly, door knob and dog leash. If we die on a clear night, stars, scattered like grains of salt across the rich, black bread of the sky, will inspire hunger, thirst.

When we die: if we die in the middle of a Leonard Cohen song, Cohen will continue to sing—*O see the darkness yielding/That tore the light apart/Come healing of the reason/Come healing of the heart*—all the way to the end of his *penitential hymn.*

If we die in our sleep, we will slip away like a lover, quietly, hoping not to disturb her, our beloved, because more than anything else in this world of pain she loves sleep and no one and nothing should trouble her when she's wrapped in sleep's arms.

If we die in a chair, the newspaper will remain open to a story growing old; if we die in a wreck, the salvageable parts of the vehicle will be salvaged and sold; if we die without hearing *I love you*, our survivors will say, for a few days, maybe a week or two, *I love you* to our favorite shirt hanging in the closet, to the clutter on top of our bureau that, until we passed, annoyed them to no end.

No, that's not what I meant, I imagine her saying, *what happens to* us *when* we *die?*

Well, then . . . I don't know. I don't know. One day, maybe 45 years ago, I thought I did.

I was in high school. I was moving in a certain direction, toward music, poetry, spirituality, art, I was moving together with friends, I was moving alone and apart. Tim Buckley, Cecil Taylor, Robert Fripp. Rauschenberg, Ginsberg, Kafka, Duchamp. I was moving in. I was moving out. Yoga, incense, pot.

Strawbridge Lake, Moorestown, New Jersey. From my house on the north side of Cherry Hill, I bicycled there alone to be alone with "nature". And I drove there with friends to walk by the water, to throw a Frisbee, to catch a glimpse of a life we longed for, we counterculture teens, a reflective life we were already living, stoned. Better there, by water and among trees, than at the Cherry Hill Mall, though we wandered there, stoned in that climate-controlled Eden, too.

One sunny afternoon, I remember, I was stoned and while two friends walked one way, and one or two others walked another, I lay on the cropped grass near the lake. And on my back I felt the cold ground and then my back melted and my body was earth all the way down to the core. And I gazed at the branches of a tree overhead and the sky through and beyond the tree and I was free, my body was light, leaf, bark, sky. No boundaries. Not even an "I" to say, to loved ones mourning my disappearance, my absence, don't be sad, I am the hot smoke you draw into your lungs and hold for a few seconds before releasing it, I am the spinning disc and its shadow moving toward your hand ready to snatch it. And I heard a voice speak, and it said *this is what happens when you die*—you live as before, before you were reduced and confined to body and voice by which others knew you. You live now as *life* itself.

An out-of-body experience, and a voice telling me, *now you know, now you need not worry about death. Get on with your life.*

But now, I don't know. And maybe, because, thank God, I haven't lost a son or daughter, I enjoy the luxury of not having to think about it.

All I know is this: if we die before 4 in the afternoon on a Tuesday in America, the stock market will continue to post losses, gains. If we die old, they will say *he lived a full life*. If we die young, before our parents, they will say, *it's not supposed to be that way* and *he died before his time*. But Time will say nothing, and Time will do nothing to ease the pain of those who question and live, who call out and wait and wait for a reply.

After Hearing That a Friend Visiting Israel for the First Time Asked Her Private Tour Guide, "Where Is the Garden of Eden?"

Where is the Garden of Eden?
Can I see it from the hotel, east-facing
room on the 18th floor?
Does the 18 bus stop there?
My children, I think,
they must have grown up
in the Garden of Eden while I was away
with work, 18 hour nights
and days. Look—their radiant
faces! Listen—their voices, sweet rivers
on which I, afloat, drift.

When I was 18, I was invited to love
for the first time. But before
I arrived at the Garden
of Eden, I spilled what I was
given to deliver. My friend
who presented herself to me
that night in my childhood
bedroom, smiled, took my hand,
and led me to the mirror to admire
our bodies reflected. She was
patient, reassuring, wise.
Did she think we would
find the Garden of Eden
in the mirror, its honey
dripping, its hive alive
with bees? Finally, we fell
back into bed in the dark.
Even if it was only
18 seconds, it was real,
almond balm, evergreen breeze,
the Garden of all dreams.

Eighteen days or was it 18
months or 18 years: how long
my recovery from first, second,
third love—loss
of the Garden?

I'm married now 18 years. For life.
Marriage is not Eden, where nothing is
broken, shattered, bent, destroyed.
Nothing to forget, nothing to recall.
But there are moments
when there is nothing
more perfect than my wife's
complaints about her day, the 18
ants that crawled on her
legs while she played
on a filthy floor in
Hidden River Trailer Park
with a 2½-year-old boy, trying
to get him to say
"p" and "b," as in "pop," "boom."
Do you remember the Garden
of Eden, I ask her, and I wait,
and I listen all night, even
long after she has fallen
asleep and I am lying
beside her as beside
the river that waters the Garden
on its way out of Eden
where it splits four ways
and spills into children's lives.

Tashlikh 5773

"And you will cast all their sins into the depth of the sea" – Micah 7

Tashlikh: a ritual of symbolically casting one's sins into a moving body of water performed on Rosh Hashanah afternoon

Into this
shallow
creek,
into this
narrow
gesture
of land,
this
slow
discourse
of water,
I empty
my holiday
pockets,
a year's
crumbs
of gossip,
I empty
my eyes
of lust,
my heart
of unsym-
pathetic joy
over his
fortune,
I empty
my hand
of the fist
and my mouth

of silence
where there
should have
been cries
of injustice,
I empty even
the emptiness
of vows I
made last
night, before
the open
heart of
this synagogue,
this wounded
house of
prayer;
into this
trickle
I empty the
comfort
of ritual
so that I
may stand
stripped to
the bone
of creation,
without
a deed
to just-
ify my
life, this
life, carried
now only
by the current
of Your mercy.

Notes

A handful of Hebrew words in transliteration are used in this book. In most cases, the transliterated words are translated into English immediately following their appearance in the text. Words that may benefit from additional explanation as well as some other useful information on the poems can be found below.

"For Love" • Page 10

Tisha B'Av, the Ninth of *Av*: Jews observe the 9th day of the Hebrew month of *Av*, the day when, according to tradition, both the First and Second Temples were destroyed, by fasting and participating in other mourning rituals.

"For Love" includes excerpts from three poems by Robert Creeley, "The Warning," "The Rain," and "For Love." I first read these poems in the paperback edition of Creeley's *For Love: Poems, 1950–1960* (Scribner, New York, 1967). The excerpts included here were taken from Creeley's *Selected Poems* (University of California Press, Berkeley, 1996).

"Make It Old: A Wedding Anniversary Epithalamion" • Page 16

Excerpts from "The Song of Songs" are taken from *The Jewish Study Bible, featuring The Jewish Publication Society Tanakh Translation.* Edited by Adele Berlin and Marc Zvi Brettler. Consulting Editor, Michael Fishbane. Oxford UP, New York, 2004.

"The *Huppah*" • Page 19

huppah: wedding canopy. At some Jewish weddings, a *tallis,* a traditional prayer shawl, is used for the canopy under which bride and groom stand during the ceremony. Some Jewish prayer shawls are white with black stripes. Others, including the prayer shawl on which this poem is based, feature stripes of many colors.

"from *The Book of Brothers*" • Page 25

See the Torah on the lives of Jacob and Esau for the context out of which "from *The Book of Brothers*" emerges. The poem is also informed by Avivah Gottlieb Zornberg's commentary on Jacob and Esau found in her book *The Beginning of Desire: Reflections on Genesis.* Image Books: Doubleday, New York, 1995.

Jacob. In Hebrew: *Ya'akov*. The commentators of *Etz Hayim: Torah and Commentary*, published by The Rabbinical Assembly and the United Synagogue of Conservative Judaism, offer the following explanation of Jacob's name. "The name is . . . derived, by folk etymology, from the Hebrew noun *akev*, heel." In Genesis, 25:26, Jacob's birth is described as follows: "Then his [Esau's] brother emerged, holding on to the heel of Esau; so they named him Jacob." The *Etz Hayim* commentators note, however, that "the Hebrew name *ya-akov* stems from a Semitic verb [*ekev*], to protect. Thus, in its origin, the name Jacob is a plea for divine protection of the newly born."

Rashi: Rashi (Rabbi Solomon Yitzchaki) is a seminal rabbinic commentator from France who lived from 1040-1105.

midrash: a rabbinic method of interpretation that includes filling in gaps in biblical narratives and other interpretive strategies.

"The Book of Brothers" • Page 32

bet: the second letter of the Hebrew alphabet.

"And Holy" • Page 35

Y-H-V-H: the four-letter, unpronounceable name of God. The letters from the English alphabet are phonetic approximations of the Hebrew letters: *yud, hey, vav, hey*.

"Confession" • Page 44

d'var Torah: a teaching based on a portion of the Torah; *haftarah:* a reading from the prophets that follows the reading from the Torah during the Jewish prayer service.

Ya'akov: see note above for "from *The Book of Brothers*."

"are you my god" • Page 52

seder: the ritual observed in Jewish families' homes on Passover.

"Enemies of Israel, Enemies of the Jews" • Page 57

Egged bus: the largest transit bus company, a cooperative owned by its members, in Israel.

IDF: Israel Defense Forces

"What I've Been Given" • Page 64

kaddish: In this case, the Jewish mourner's prayer.

"Tashlikh" • Page 72

This ceremony on the afternoon of the first day of Rosh Hashanah symbolically enacts the casting away of one's sins in the form of bread crumbs or lint from one's pockets into a moving body of water.

Acknowledgments

Thanks to the editors who published some of the work (sometimes in earlier versions) included in this book.

The Forward: "The Ways of Gods and Women" (originally entitled "Rachel and The Household Gods")

Image: "The Other Face of Adam" (originally entitled "When God Dreamed Eve Through Adam"), "The Book of Brothers," "After Hearing That a Friend Visiting Israel for the First Time Asked Her Private Tour Guide, "Where Is the Garden Of Eden?" and "are you my god"

Literature and Belief: "Mezuzah"

New England Review: "To Be Read Before Reciting the Blessing for the Washing of the Hands" (originally entitled "Say Hands")

St. Katherine's Review: "The Huppah"

Smartish Pace: "The Rest Is Prayer" (originally titled "At the Table of the Lord")

Far from the Centers of Ambition, Lorimer Press: "For Love"

"Good Letters," a blog hosted by *Image* and *Patheos*: "Make It Old: A Wedding Anniversary Epithalamion"; 'How God Came To Be God"; "Enemies of Israel, Enemies of the Jews"; "His Murderer *and* His Keeper"; "Dear Time"; "Hide and Seek"; "What I've Been Given"; "When We Die"; "The Poems Left In Me"

Good Noticing, Institute of Jewish Spirituality: "Re: Writing Torah" (in a significantly different version)

* * * *

The work gathered in this book was written in the midst of life, not while stepping away and setting myself apart from its demands, opportunities, pleasures, frustrations, struggles, disappointments, rewards. This work grew from the heart of life itself—work, family, exercise and play, community, social, and spiritual life. As such, there are many people to thank for their role in creating the conditions that have made this work possible.

In recent years, my life—as a Jew, an educator, a husband and father, a congregant, a friend, a writer—has been deepened and widened thanks to the discipline of contemplative practice. Rabbis Jeff Roth, Sheila Peltz-Weinberg, and Jordan Bendat-Appell have been my teachers on the path of Jewish contemplative life. And my ongoing practice of contemplative Judaism has been strengthened and steadied by my work with my *hevruta* partner, Rabbi Batsheva Meiri.

About six years ago, I received an invitation from Greg Wolfe, publisher and editor of the journal *Image*, to become a regular contributor to the journal's blog "Good Letters." The platform and freedom—as well as the deadlines!—Greg gave me have done nothing less than transform my writing. "Good Letters" has also enabled me to reach generous, supportive readers who otherwise might never have stumbled across my work. Thank you, Greg, and Mary Kenagy Mitchell, managing editor of *Image*, Cathy Warner and Jan Vallone, the two editors of the blog "Good Letters," and Peggy Rosenthal, another long time contributor to "Good Letters." Your encouragement and support have made it possible for me to grow as a writer and a man.

About six years ago, I was fortunate to be chosen as UNC Asheville's first Roy Carroll Professor of Honors Arts & Sciences. Thank you, Ed Katz! The appointment comes with some release time from teaching in order to develop and implement a project to benefit UNC Asheville. My project is to introduce, encourage, and provide support for the use of contemplative practices in the classroom and throughout the university. My work on this project, and the professional friendships—at my own institution and beyond—I've developed through this work have also been invaluable to me and have nourished me as a writer as well as in many other ways. Thank you to my contemplative community in higher education, especially Eva Bares, Ameena Batada, Ken Betsalel, Pat Foo, Melissa Mahoney, Keya Maitra, Sonia Marcus, John Wood, and Kate Zubko at UNC Asheville, and Daniel Barbezat, Carrie Bergman, David Levy, Judith Simmer-Brown, and Patricia Wallace—colleagues and friends from the Center for Contemplative Mind.

To my friends who have faith in literature, thank you!

Richard Mathews—your commitment to my work has truly changed my life. Your dedication to University of Tampa Press and the work you've done to design and publish so many gorgeous books and so much good writing will continue to benefit others for many, many years. Thank you, Richard.

Don Morrill: you have been with me from the first day of graduate school, when you encouraged me to read Jonathan Holden's *The Rhetoric of the*

Contemporary Lyric, to this very day, always a teacher, always a writer whose work serves as an inspiration to me, always a dear friend. You were the first to encourage me to submit work to *Tampa Review*, and since my first publication there, Tampa has been a home for my work. Thank you.

Alice, Margaret, and Gabe, Farbod and Shuchin, Ilia, Hassan, Abraham, and Maya—children and step-children, sons-in-law, and grandchildren: I hope I have given you a small portion of what I receive from you and your commitment to creating—through your professional lives and the way you attend to your own growing families—a more just, loving, and kind world—a borderless world.

Laurie, dear wife, best friend, source of strength and wisdom, patient with me when patience is best for both of us, challenging me when, in your wisdom, I need to be challenged for my own and our benefit, nothing I have accomplished in the last twenty-eight years would have been possible without you.

About the Author and Artist

Richard Chess is the author of four books of poetry, *Love Nailed to the Doorpost* (University of Tampa Press 2017), *Tekiah* (University of Georgia Press 1996; republished by University of Tampa Press 2000); *Chair in the Desert* (University of Tampa Press 2000); and *Third Temple* (University of Tampa Press 2006). His poems have appeared in *Best American Spiritual Writing 2005*, *Telling and Remembering: A Century of American Jewish Poetry*, and *The Bloomsbury Anthology of Contemporary American Jewish Poetry*. He has also published essays in *27 Views of Asheville* (Eno Publishers 2012) and *The Carolina Table: North Carolina Writers on Food* (Eno Publishers 2016). He is a regular contributor to "Good Letters," the blog hosted by *Image Journal.*

He is an award-winning professor at the University of North Carolina Asheville, where he chairs the English Department. He has served as director of UNC Asheville's Center for Jewish Studies since 1992. In recent years, he has become active in the national movement exploring the use of contemplative pedagogy in higher education. He has served on the faculty of the Association for Contemplative Mind in Higher Education (ACMHE) Summer Seminar in Contemplative Pedagogy Development (2015), and he has presented every year since 2011 at the annual ACMHE Academic Conference. At UNC Asheville, he has played a leading role in the contemplative pedagogy and practice initiative which began there in 2011.

Daniel Nevins is an artist known for figurative and abstract compositions connoting a sense of spiritual embodiment. His work has been seen all over the world and reviewed in publications as diverse as *The New York Times, The Wall Street Journal*, and *Hi-Fructose* magazine. He recently illustrated a re-telling of the Torah entitled *With a Mighty Hand: The Story in the Torah*, published by Candlewick Press. When not painting, he plays guitar in a rock band and is currently pursuing a graduate degree in psychotherapy from Lenoir-Rhyne University. He lives in Asheville, North Carolina.

About the Book

Love Nailed to the Doorpost is set in Adobe Garamond Pro, a digital font developed from the sixteenth century roman types of Claude Garamond and the italics of Robert Granjon. Adobe Systems type designer Robert Slimbach visited the Plantin-Moretus Museum in Antwerp, Belgium, for research while working on the font. He later wrote, "The experience of studying near flawless proofs of Garamond's and Granjon's types was a revelation which led to a major overhaul of the working design." Slimbach's original digital fonts, released in 1989, have been further refined with digital options available in the newer Open Type format. The result is a versatile and highly readable serif face that preserves the grace and proportion of classical letterforms while projecting a timeless and contemporary clarity. The book was designed and typeset by Richard Mathews at the University of Tampa Press.